Animals
Without
Backbones

Elaine Pascoe
Photographs by Dwight Kuhn

Published in 2003 by The Rosen Publishing Group, Inc.
29 East 21st Street, New York, NY 10010

First Edition

Editor: Natashya Wilson
Book Design: Emily Muschinske

Photo Credits: All photographs © Dwight Kuhn, except page 10 © Stephen Frink/CORBIS.

Pascoe, Elaine.
Animals without backbones / Elaine Pascoe.
    p. cm. — (A kid's guide to the classification of living things)
Includes bibliographical references (p.   ).
Summary: Describes the physical characteristics, behavior, and habitat of animals that do not have internal skeletal systems.
  ISBN 0-8239-6311-X (lib. bdg.)
1. Invertebrates—Classification—Juvenile literature. [1. Invertebrates.] I. Title.
  QL362.4 .P37 2003
  592—dc21

                                                          2001006644

Manufactured in the United States of America

Contents

Kingdoms of Life

How is a snail like a bee? How are they different? Scientists ask such questions when they classify living things. Just as you might sort forks and spoons in a drawer, scientists sort living things based on ways in which they are alike.

Many scientists sort living things into five **kingdoms**. The diagram to the right shows how the animal kingdom is sorted into smaller groups. All creatures in a kingdom are alike in some ways. Animals make up one kingdom. All animals can move from one place to another, and all animals find and eat food.

This book is about one branch of the animal kingdom, animals without backbones. Let's see what kinds of animals can be sorted into this group.

Each kingdom can be sorted into more specific groups. In this diagram the animal kingdom is sorted into single types of animals without backbones.

Plant Kingdom

Fungus Kingdom

Animal Kingdom

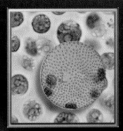

Protist Kingdom

Monera Kingdom

Animals Without Backbones

Animals With Backbones

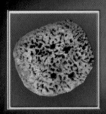

Sponges

Worms

Echinoderms

Mollusks

Arthropods

Honeybee

Green-Headed Horsefly

Giant Hairy Hadrurus Scorpion

Luna Moth

5

Bones and No Bones

Bones give your body shape. They also protect important body parts. For example, bones called **vertebrae** make up your backbone. They protect the **spinal cord**, a bundle of **nerves** that connects your brain with the rest of your body.

Many animals don't have backbones. In fact many animals have no bones at all. Because they have no backbones, or vertebrae, these animals are called **invertebrates**. Among them are animals as different from each other as the jellyfish and the butterfly.

There are many different kinds of invertebrates. In fact 90 percent of all animals are invertebrates! By looking at invertebrates' traits, you can sort them into smaller groups, as do scientists.

 Top: *A mouse is an animal with a backbone.* Bottom: *A snail is an invertebrate. It has a soft body that is protected by a hard shell.*

Sponges: Simplest of All

Have you ever washed with a natural sponge? You were using the **skeleton** of an ocean animal! The bath sponge is one of about 5,000 kinds of sponges. Sponges come in all shapes and sizes. Some are soft, such as the bath sponge. Some are stiff.

A sponge has no brain, no heart, and no legs. It eats by pulling water into small openings, called **pores**, all over its body. The sponge filters tiny bits of food from the water. You can tell a sponge by its pores, and by the honeycomb structure of its body.

Sponges spend most of their lives stuck to one spot. They swim only when they are first born, as tiny **larvae**. Sponges are the simplest group of animals without backbones.

This bath sponge is the skeleton of an ocean animal. When it was alive, it pulled in water and food through the pores in its body.

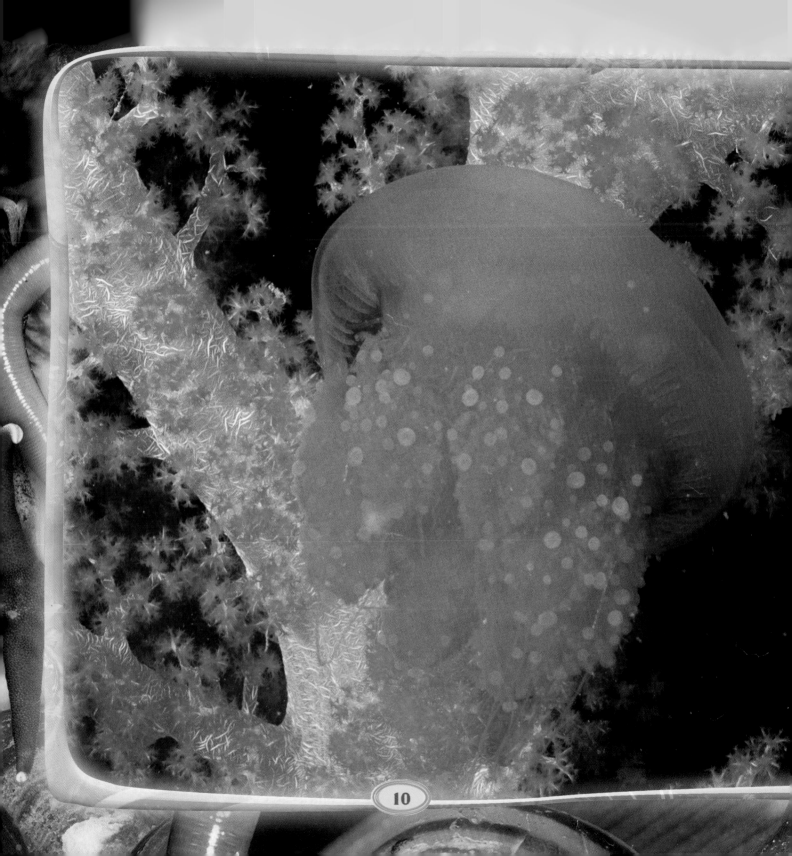

Jellyfish: Watery Stingers

A jellyfish is another invertebrate. Its body looks like a clump of jelly. Most jellyfish live in the ocean. Jellyfish and their relatives have stinging, armlike parts, called **tentacles**, around their mouths. They sting to stun their **prey**, such as small fish or tiny animals that look like shrimp. Then they sweep the prey into their mouths.

Sea anemones, corals, and freshwater animals called hydras are closely related to jellyfish. The sea anemone's sting is poisonous. Like the jellyfish, the sea anemone stuns small fish and eats them. Its sting doesn't bother one kind of fish, the clownfish. A clownfish can live right among the tentacles. It is safe from **predators** there.

 Jellyfish are 95 percent water. They do not have hearts, blood, brains, or gills. However, they are able to sense things around them.

Sponges may come in many shapes and colors, but they all have pores. This is a free-standing sponge.

These sponges, called bread-and-crumbs sponges, live in tide pools at the edge of an ocean.

Clownfish use sea anemones for protection and to get food. The fish eat the leftovers of the anemone's meals.

A sea anemone often will attach itself to rock or coral. It is able to move slowly, however.

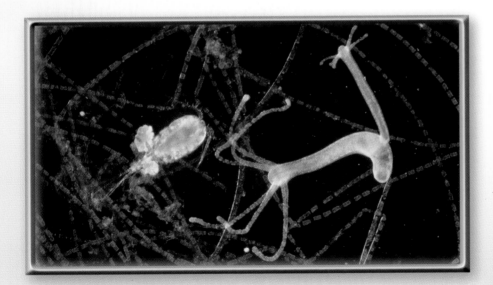

Like jellyfish and sea anemones, hydras have stinging tentacles. This brown hydra is about to eat a small animal.

Worms: Wriggly Workers

Worms are also invertebrates. They are simple animals. Food goes in the front end. Wastes go out the back. Only a few types of worms have eyes.

Earthworms are one kind of worm. An earthworm's body is made up of little rings, or segments. Earthworms tunnel through soil, eating bits of dead plants and animals. As they tunnel, they let air and water into the soil. This helps plants to grow.

There are other types of worms as well. Roundworms are long and smooth, with no segments. Flatworms are flat, like ribbons. Many roundworms and flatworms are **parasites**. They live inside other animals and feed on them. These two types of worms belong to separate invertebrate groups.

Earthworms live all around the world. As they tunnel in the ground, they turn the soil. Their tunnels allow air and water to reach the roots of plants.

Common American earthworms have about 150 segments.

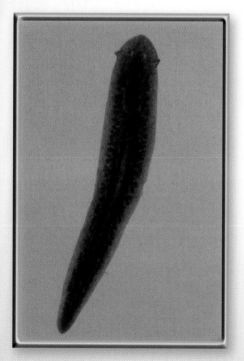

A planarian is a kind of flatworm. It lives in freshwater and eats rotting meat.

Roundworms, such as this one, are parasites. They can be found in the intestines of pigs and humans. They can grow to be 18 inches (46 cm) long.

This is a close-up view of a tapeworm's head. Tapeworms are part of the flatworm group. They live in animals' stomachs or intestines and feed on food that the animals eat.

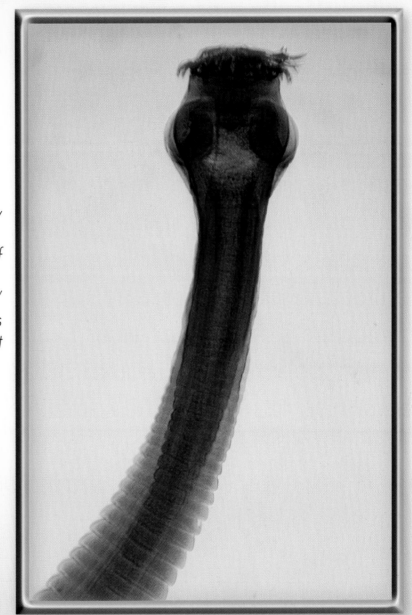

Echinoderms: Spiny Stars

Sea stars are sometimes called starfish. They are not fish, however. They are invertebrates called echinoderms. "Echinoderm" means "spiny-skinned." Almost all echinoderms have tough skin on their bodies, as well as stiff spines. Sea stars and sand dollars are covered with tiny spines. Sea urchins can have much longer spines.

Echinoderms are put together in a balanced way. Most echinoderms have regular, five-sided shapes. A sea star's arms are all the same. They all grow out from the center of its body. At the tip of each arm is a tiny eye! A sea star wraps its arms around a clam and pries the shell open. Then it eats the soft animal inside.

A sea star, such as this blood star, can regrow most of its body if it is damaged. If ⅕ of the center and 1 arm remain, a sea star can completely regrow. The whole process can take up to 1 year.

Mollusks: Snails and More

What does a garden snail have in common with a clam or an octopus? These animals are invertebrates called **mollusks**. Mollusks have soft bodies. Most have shells made of a hard material that their bodies **secrete**. They also have feet, although their feet may be hard to spot.

A snail has one foot, on its underside. The snail glides along on its foot, leaving a little trail of slime. The feet of the octopus are on its tentacles. The octopus uses its tentacles to catch prey. Even a clam has a foot, although clams hardly ever move. A clam can stick its foot out of its shell to push itself away from danger.

This is a land snail on a leaf. The snail moves by secreting slime from its foot and sliding along at a very slow pace.

A slug is closely related to a snail, but a slug does not have a hard shell.

Mussels are mollusks that live in either freshwater or salt water. These are saltwater mussels.

Sea urchins are members of the echinoderm group. They are covered with stiff spines.

Like sea stars and sea urchins, sand dollars are echinoderms. The pattern on the top of this sand dollar skeleton shows the 5-sided shape. Live sand dollars are brownish purple.

Arthropods: Lots of Legs

Can you spot the ways in which a crab and a spider are alike? Both of these animals have many jointed legs. Crabs and spiders are invertebrates called **arthropods**. "Arthropod" means "jointed foot."

Arthropods are alike in other ways as well. Their bodies are divided into segments, or sections. Most arthropods have hard outer coats, or **exoskeletons**, to protect the soft insides of their bodies.

Spiders have four pairs of legs. Centipedes and millipedes have many pairs of legs. The front legs of crabs, lobsters, and crayfish have pincers for grasping food. The scorpion also has pincers, plus a stinger on its tail. All of these animals are arthropods.

The body segments and jointed legs that mark an arthropod can be seen in this picture of a millipede.

Arthropods: Insects

Insects are a group within the arthropod group. There are more types, or **species**, of insects than any other type of animal. Scientists know of more than 750,000 species of insects. There may be millions more. Bees, ladybugs, flies, grasshoppers, and mosquitoes are just a few of the many types of insects.

Insects come in all shapes and sizes. Some moths have wings more than 10 inches (25 cm) across! Insects can fly, hop, or crawl. All insects have three pairs of jointed legs and three body sections.

Most insects have good senses. Their **compound eyes** have many lenses, so they can see in all directions at the same time. Insects can smell, taste, and feel with the antennae, or feelers, on their heads.

Insects, such as this horsefly, have huge compound eyes made up of many tiny lenses. This allows insects to see in all directions at once.

A rock crab is an arthropod. It has two large pincers on its front legs.

Spiders, such as this red-legged tarantula, have eight legs and two main body parts.

The segmented body, jointed legs, and exoskeleton of this crayfish show that it is an arthropod.

The short-horned grasshopper eats plants. Like all insects, it has six legs and three body sections.

The luna moth lives in eastern North America. Its wings can measure 4 inches (10 cm) across.

A honeybee is part of the insect group. It collects nectar, spreads pollen from flower to flower, and makes honey.

Living or Not?

Like the members of all the kingdoms, animals without backbones are living things. Look around. How many living things do you see? Trees, birds, insects, and fish are different, but they all have some things in common.

All living things, from snails to people, grow and develop. They **reproduce**, or make more of their own kind. A snail lays eggs that hatch into new snails. A flower forms seeds that grow into new plants. Living things use food. Plants make their own food. Animals get their food in many ways. Living things sense the world around them and react to it. Even plants do this. In all these ways, living things are different from nonliving things.

Although many creatures live in them, water and sand are nonliving things.

Glossary

arthropods (AR-thruh-podz) The scientific name for a group of animals with jointed legs and hard outer coverings.

compound eyes (KOM-pownd EYEZ) Eyes that have many lenses.

exoskeletons (ek-soh-SKEH-leh-tinz) Hard, tough coverings on the outsides of animals' bodies that support and protect the soft insides.

invertebrates (in-VER-tih-brits) Animals with no backbones.

kingdoms (KEENG-duhmz) The first level of groups into which scientists sort living things.

larvae (LAHR-vee) The early life stage of certain animals.

mollusks (MAH-lusks) A group of animals with soft bodies and, often, shells.

nerves (NERVZ) Body tissues that carry information between the brain and the other parts of the body.

parasites (PAR-uh-syts) Living things that live and feed in or on other living things.

pores (PORZ) Small openings in the body surface.

predators (PREH-duh-terz) Animals that hunt and eat other animals.

prey (PRAY) An animal that is hunted by another animal for food.

reproduce (ree-pruh-DOOS) To have babies.

secrete (sih-KREET) To make a substance inside the body then let it out.

skeleton (SKEH-lih-tun) The set of bones in an animal's body.

species (SPEE-sheez) The smallest grouping in the classification of living things.

spinal cord (SPY-nuhl KORD) A long bundle of nerves that runs down the back.

tentacles (TEN-tuh-kulz) Long, thin growths, usually on the head or near the mouths of animals, used to touch, to hold, or to move.

vertebrae (VEHR-tuh-bray) Backbones, which protect the spinal cord.

Index

Web Sites

Due to the changing nature of Internet links, PowerKids Press has developed an online list of Web sites related to the subject of this book. This site is updated regularly. Please use this link to access the list:
www.powerkidslinks.com/kgclt/anwobb/